I0824506

Level Up Gaming

LEVEL UP FORTNITE

LORI DITTMER

BLACK RABBIT BOOKS

Bolt is published by Black Rabbit Books
P.O. Box 227, Mankato, Minnesota, 56002.
www.blackrabbitbooks.com

BOLT

Alissa Thielges, editor; Rhea Magaro, designer and photo researcher

Library of Congress Cataloging-in-Publication Data
Names: Dittmer, Lori author
Title: Level up Fortnite / by Lori Dittmer.
Description: Mankato, MN : Black Rabbit Books, [2026] | Series: Level up gaming | Includes bibliographical references and index. | Audience: Ages 8-12 | Audience: Grades 4-6
Identifiers: LCCN 2025017493 (print) | LCCN 2025017494 (ebook) | ISBN 9781645824756 library binding | ISBN 9781645824831 ebook
Subjects: LCSH: Fortnite video games—Juvenile literature
Classification: LCC GV1469.35.F67 D58 2026 (print) | LCC GV1469.35.F67 (ebook) | DDC 794.8—dc23/eng/20250621
LC record available at https://lccn.loc.gov/2025017493
LC ebook record available at https://lccn.loc.gov/2025017494

Printed in China

Image Credits

Dreamstime/Aksitaykut, 24; Getty Images/Benedikt Wenck/picture alliance, 24; Epic Games, cover, 1, 3, 4–5, 6, 7, 8, 11, 12, 13, 14, 15, 16, 17, 18, 20, 21, 23, 27, 28, 31, 32; Shutterstock/AI Generator, cover, 9, icon0.com, 25, jamesteohart, 7, lazy_leric, 27, Oleh Veres, 26.

Every effort has been made to contact copyright holders for material reproduced in this book. Any omissions will be rectified in subsequent printings if notice is given to the publisher.

CONTENTS

CHAPTER 1

ALL ABOARD

A boy selects *Fortnite Battle Royale* **mode**. He goes to Spawn Island. He picks up a weapon. Soon, everyone is ready. They step onto the Battle Bus. It flies through the sky. Then, the boy jumps. As he lands, he sees a chest. Great! He grabs the **loot**. He is ready to fight!

Each *Battle Royale* game lasts about 20 minutes.

GAME MODES

Save the World

Battle Royale

Creative

LEGO Fortnite

Fortnite Battle Royale

Fortnite is a third-person shooting game. Epic Games released it 2017. Players can choose from several modes. The most popular is *Fortnite Battle Royale*. In this game, 100 players are on an island. They fight the other players. The last one standing is the winner. Many people play **solo**. Players can also team up in teams of two or four.

Rocket Racing

CHAPTER 2

STARTING OUT

Players drop to the island from the flying bus. They look for weapons. A pickaxe will hit trees, walls, and cars. These items break down into wood, stone, and metal. Players use these to build **forts** and ramps. But everyone must keep moving to the center of the island. While the battle roars, a storm grows. It slowly shrinks the playing area.

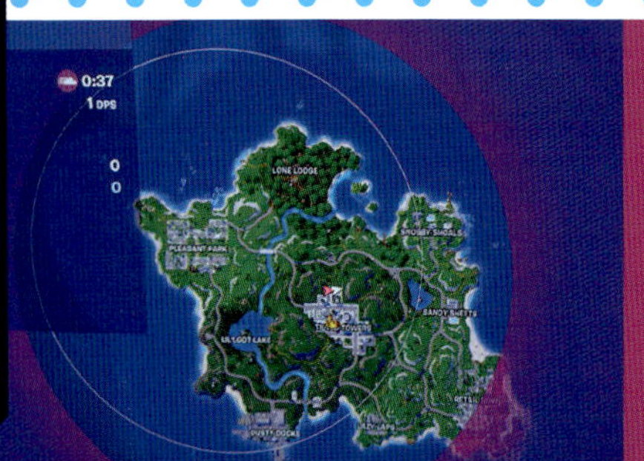

The safe zone is the eye of the storm. It grows smaller during the game. This pushes players together.

BY THE NUMBERS

650 million

NUMBER OF PEOPLE WHO HAVE SIGNED UP TO PLAY AS OF 2025.

30 million

Number of active users per day in 2024.

September 26, 2017

Date *Fortnite Battle Royale* came out.

14,343,880

All-time high number of people playing at the same time.

Stats and More

Weapons and items are hidden around the island. There are several types. Each one glows. The color shows its strength. Sometimes there are special items. These might be crossbows or grenade launchers. They are hard to find. First aid kits and shield potions are helpful. Each player can hold five items at a time.

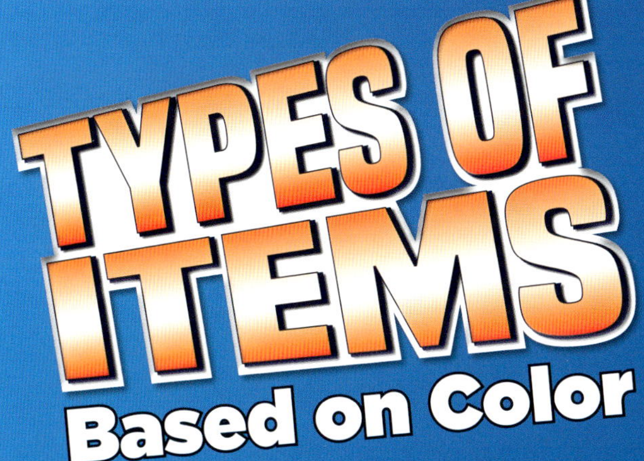
TYPES OF ITEMS
Based on Color

Common

Uncommon

Rare

Epic

Legendary

Mythic

Exotic

150 150
EDIT

Building Structures

Players use **resources** to build. Wood is the weakest. But wooden structures are the fastest to build. Metal is the strongest. Buildings give players a better view of the island. This helps to find enemies or loot. If players are hurt, they build forts. These protect against attacks while they heal.

A boogie bomb forces another player to dance for five seconds.

Players use dance moves to celebrate a win. They dance to make fun of enemies. Popular dances are Griddy or You Think You the King.

Building Experience

Fortnite Battle Royale is free to play. Money in the game is called V-bucks. It can be earned by completing quests. V-bucks buy outfits, or "skins." They also buy dance moves, called emotes.

Players also build experience points (XP). Playing LEGO Fortnite earns 46,000 XP every 15 minutes. Daily quests lead to XP too. Collecting XP unlocks rewards.

CHAPTER 3

LEARNING THE MAP

Battle Royale has several chapters. Each one has a story and theme. Popular themes have been superheroes, aliens, and Star Wars. The island map changes too. Players can improve by studying the map. The more they play, the more they learn the layout.

SNOBBY SANDS
FOSSIL FIELDS
LIZARD LINKS
ADOBE ABODES
PARADISE PALMS
TS
GUACO TOWN
SHADY SPRINGS

TALKING TO NPCS

Many non-player characters (NPCs) roam the island.

UNFRIENDLY
ATTACK PLAYERS

MIDAS

ORELIA

CUBE ASSASSIN

ANIMALS
HELPFUL

BOARS

CHICKENS

ALIEN PARASITES

CHAPTER 4

MASTERING THE GAME

Battle Royale puts players together based on their skills. Some players might be **bots**. This keeps the games fair. Ranked play is harder. Players move up ranks by winning games. They can also complete challenges. Both earn points. The average player rank is silver or gold.

FORTNITE RANKED

Rank	I	II	III
BRONZE			
SILVER			
GOLD			
PLATINUM			
DIAMOND			
ELITE			
CHAMPION			
UNREAL			

FORTNITE
CIRCLE NUMBER 2/9
STORM CLOCK 1:32
PLAYERS REMAINING 78/100
SCARLET
WADE

Professional Esport

Fortnite is a popular **esport**. Many schools have teams. Players with high ranks might go pro. They compete in top competitions. One is the Esports World Cup. Sixteen teams battle for victory. *Fortnite* Championship Series is another big competition. The top 50 teams face off.

Practice, practice, practice.
Pro gamers play 5 to 10 hours per day.

Build hand-eye skills.
Try to increase your speed.

Improve your aim.
Practice shooting in Creative mode.

Watch others play.
Follow pros who **stream** their play online.

Bugha
(Kyle Giersdorf)
$3.7 million

Aqua
(David Wang)
$2.2 million

Psalm
(Harrison Chang)
$1.96 million

EpikWhale
(Shane Cotton)
$1.84 million

Changing Challenges

Fortnite Battle Royale was an instant hit. It has kept its place as one of the most popular games. It is free to play. Even though it is a shooting game, it is not bloody. And the cartoon images make it fun. New maps bring more challenges. Players must think and act quickly. They battle to be the last one standing in a thrilling victory.

GLOSSARY

bot (BOT)—a computer program that is designed to do tasks on its own

esport (EE-spawrt)—competitive video gaming

fort (FOHRT)—a strong building or group of buildings where fighters live

loot (LOOT)—valuable items that can be claimed from a defeated enemy or chest

mode (MOHD)—a set of rules within a game that changes how it is played

resource (REE-sohrs)—a concept or element that can be measured or counted and is controlled by the player

solo (SOH-loh)—something that is done without another person

stream (STREEM)—to send or receive video or audio material over the internet in a steady flow

BOOKS

Abdo, Kenny. *Fortnite*. Mankato, MN: Abdo Publishing, 2023.

Downs, Kieran. *Fortnite*. Minneapolis: Bellwether Media, 2024.

Storm, Marysa. *Battle Royale Games*. Mankato, MN: Black Rabbit Books, 2026.

WEBSITES

Fortnite
www.fortnite.com

Fortnite Facts for Kids
kids.kiddle.co/Fortnite

INDEX